Wandering Off

NATURE'S NOTABLE NOURISHMENTS

JEANNIE O. HARSHA &
TRICIA NICKERSON

Balboa Press books may be ordered through booksellers or by contacting:

Balboa Press
A Division of Hay House
1663 Liberty Drive
Bloomington, IN 47403
www.balboapress.com
1 (877) 407-4847

Because of the dynamic nature of the Internet, any web addresses or links contained in this book may have changed since publication and may no longer be valid. The views expressed in this work are solely those of the author and do not necessarily reflect the views of the publisher, and the publisher hereby disclaims any responsibility for them.

Poems by Jeannie O. Harsha
Photos by Tricia Nickerson

ISBN: 978-1-9822-3348-8 (sc)
ISBN: 978-1-9822-3349-5 (e)

Library of Congress Control Number: 2019912425

Print information available on the last page.

Balboa Press rev. date: 08/24/2019

BALBOA.
PRESS
A DIVISION OF HAY HOUSE

To all who've walked a path with me and shared stories around campfires or the kitchen table; and to those who yet will. And to my family, my precious gems.

Jeannie O. Harsha

Enjoy!
Jeannie O. Harsha

To my Babe and best friend: Thank you for encouraging me on my artistic journey and for your constant, loving support. To my daughter: Love you to the moon and beyond! To loving family members and treasured friends.

Tricia Nickerson

May your heart be
filled with the
wonders of nature!
Tricia Nickerson

A Tiny Seed

A tiny seed is all
it takes to prove
the miracle of growth

A tiny seed coaxed
with care
germinates, sprouts,
stretches upward

What is the tiny seed
your heart nourishes?
Allow it to germinate,
gather support
for proper expression

Love moves on the
waters of our mind
to heal, to open
to grow toward a
better world

Passion, guided rightly
takes root
and thrives

It brings down walls,
opens doors to honorable ideas,
weeds out discord

And flourishes

A bright flash

       awoke me in the wee hours
followed by rolling thunder,
driving hail, strong winds
sending wind chimes into crescendo

So nice to snuggle with my cat and my mate
in warm bed during dramatic
storm symphonies

Morning revealed cumulus
clouds pouring over yonder ridge
while those more elevated sprawled
with the wind, sailing
lickity-split to the east

Soon everything settled to a gentle
breeze; blue sky pockets opening
with a tease of sunshine
       as spring rolls into
this spot of heaven on earth

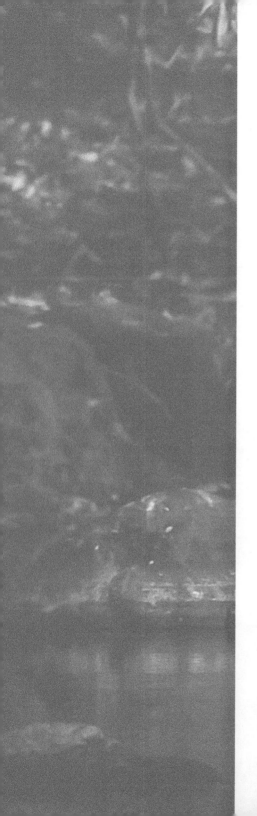

Still morning dawn

Slope of ridge on horizon
Silhouette of pine
Pale sky lightly brushed
with ashen cirrus

Scrub Jay calls three times
then quiets
a light breeze buffets boughs
outside my window

And the Great Blue Heron
lifts off the pond on silent wings

A new day begins

Quiet morning walk

                interrupted
by "pit-pit" alarm call

As a covey of quail
parade down
a freshly cut ponderosa

Three pairs,
            then six –
Soon 12 pairs of tiny feet speeding
down the log
            top knots swaying

This flurry of dappled
feathers chirps it's magic spell
            lightening the day
with cuteness

Cathedrals

Hikers love
  The Church of the Higher Elevation
Peak experiences fill one with awe;
beauty inspires

A beach walker spots a
  Cathedral in the
twenty-foot
wave curl; the choir of seabirds accompanied by
Surf's percussion section

Here in the foothills
  an early spring
stuns walkers with carpets of purple,
rose and white florals; textures and varieties so
expertly constructed

On a busy street in the city
  A sparrow
grabs a crumb from the sandwich a teen
hands off to a homeless man

Cathedrals of beauty
  and love await everywhere
For the opening eye

The morning sun

      broke through
      the fog
and the ponderosa
glistened

The mind's constant chatter
      was silenced
      by a pause
with
beauty

Just Another Day

Tranquil dawn; a few early chirpers
Coffee brewing
Fridge on low percussion
Hushed and gentle moments

Just another day:
Pines silhouetted
In gray-blue sky
Against curve of yonder ridge
Boughs swaying
In easy morning breeze

Just another day:
Deer tiptoeing into yard
Cat scouting from deck post
Tom turkeys warming up for the concert
Neighbors motorcycle revving for morning commute

Just another day:
Things to do; chores to complete
people expecting results
And the beckoning boughs wave
As I take in the minutia
That launches this day

Field Trip

Jostling, chattering 7-year olds
settle onto a log,
open their journals
and begin to write and sketch –
sights and sounds.

One wanders off to explore,
finding bright orange mold on rotting log.
Two others help the log speed up
decomposition.
Soon little feet surround brilliant green –
a praying mantis walks the path as
chattering voices work into awe.

Carefully side-stepping,
we move on to visit the turtles
sunning on logs; reflecting reptilian
profiles in gentle water.

Later, pint-size bundles of energy
settle onto duff and dried leaves;
leaning against giant oaks, making
leaf rubbings and drawings.
Two students read poignant,
pure poems about rocks and trees;
another watches an inchworm measuring
her leg.

The leaves crunch beneath our feet
as we wander back through oak-filtered
sunlight.

Kids and nature;
The nature of kids.

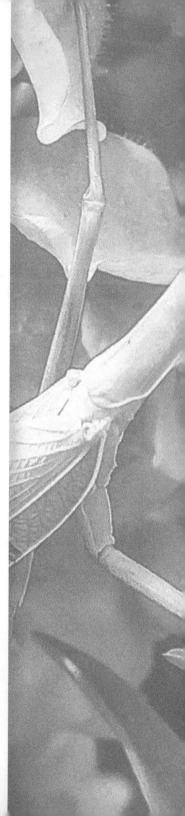

FOG

With the dawn's easy light
the fog drifted in.

I watched as it rolled over
the ridge and down pine-covered
hills, enveloping our neighbors barn;
tiptoeing across the lane to include our meadow, deck,
and dwelling.

Now I'm within a stratus cloud –
reminding me of youthful
pleasures and imaginations:
Cloud watching and wondering
what it'd be like to float
on a soft magic
carpet above blue-green Earth

How far I've come
from daydreaming days

Yet – as I sit in window-facing chair
snuggly wrapped in cloud-soft blanket,
hands nestling morning joe,
Fragrance misting my face;
Mimicking the outdoor scene…

I feel a familiar comfort:
contentment, wonder, and…
        possibility

Notable Moments

My mother remembers a bluebird
On a fence in the meadow
Where my father proposed

I remember a childhood camping trip
When brother and I snuck up to a beaver pond,
Watched them work and felt the awakening of wonder.

Perching on rocks is a pastime that evokes
Conversations and meditation in high places;
Grounded on granite or shale.

Sunrises, sunsets
Rainbows and moon phases
Move us; mend us

As do animal moments – Watching bees on flowers,
Grouse displaying on mountain trail,
A fox tail disappearing into the wood;
Gazing into the eye of a whale.

A child's laughter and energy,
A teen's incomparable humor,
A matriarch's knowing comfort,
Spread the blanket of warmth.

Today my daughter will remember
Bison snorting and cavorting beneath the Teton Range
As her lover unrolled
A blanket with a bottle of wine and a ring.

Meadow and Mountains,
Bluebirds and Bison;
Backdrops for the sweetest
Moments in time.

Lunar Eclipse

The moon was blood-red
in the wee hours of morning
as we stumbled in our jammies
to the back lawn and found
a viewing spot, unimpeded by
Ponderosa.

The news had declared:
Super moon, Blue moon, Lunar eclipse –
all on this January night!

Gazing upward towards starry sky
we watched it darken;
its edges rimmed by light.

Now, barely aware of distant rooster call,
the howling of neighborhood hounds,
the remote blink of an overnight flight…

    transfixed on this patch of earth,
we gaze together
    at our shadowy moon

Morning Magic

Only the cat and me
with eyes wide open;
one set yellow; one set blue,
       gaze into the dawn

What does she see
that I don't?
What does she hear
that I miss?

No matter – we each enjoy the stillness,
moments of calm glory
before even the early birds peep,
before lawnmowers roar to life
and school children hustle to the bus.
Like a deep soothing breath,
we take it all in.

      Daylight creeps
over the hills, touching tops
of pine; as the light gently
spreads, the sky turns pink.
Chickens flap awake, a rooster calls
and the neighborhood stirs.

The cat and I share a look.
Then she leaps off my lap
and wanders off
to explore the new day

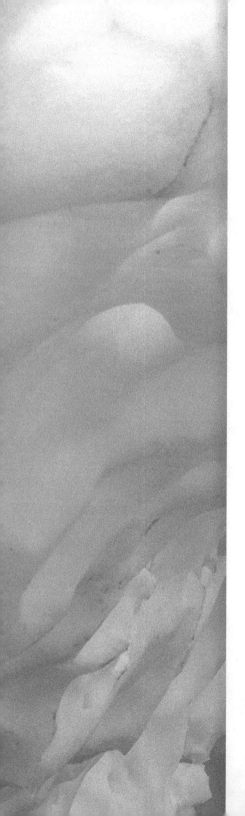

Sights and Sounds

The gibbous moon
peers through the evening clouds
on the Colorado Trail

Our tents, set up quickly
before impending rain,
billow gently in the breeze

Night Hawks are performing:
     In all my life I've
     heard one or two
But this - an incredible
symphony!

We've camped in the Night
Hawk Coliseum, paying the price
with a 15-mile hike
and delayed slumber

Strolling up ridge to
view the sunset – a Night
Hawk pair plays the broken-wing
game to draw me from their nest

Taking in their antics as
a blessing, I leave them
in peace
to absorb the beauty of western sky
the music of this mountain valley
in the light of
a lopsided moon

Teach your children

to watch the morning sun
See how it sparkles the pine boughs
Moving with the rhythm of the breeze

Teach your children
to observe the cloud variety
as they move across the skies:
cirrus, cumulus, stratus; each foretelling a pattern
Part of the wild, electric whole

Teach your children
to value the bug on the grass blade;
the bee on the blossom; the beetle
on the wall; it's apparatus flawless in structure
and design for it's place on the planet

Teach your children
to gaze at sunsets;
each evening a masterpiece
free for the viewing; subtle change
In color as darkness sets in

Teach your children
to stare in wonder
at night's starry skies; learn the
constellation stories; watch for comets
and falling stars

For then your children will be set for life
with tools of gratitude and wonder; compassion
and passion for the beauty and the order
of this world

Lunar Allure

Little crescent moon
can I follow you
across the northern sky?
You look so fine
and carefree there
among the stars so high.

Where do you go
when you drop below
yonder alpine ridge?
Is you journey bright
as you follow the light
of the biggest star we know?

I gaze at you from bedrock perch
above the shimmering river.
Your reflection is like precious gems
worth more than gold and silver.

How I long to see
what you do see
above our world so grand;
mists flowing through
our oceans blue,
spinning bulwark
securely stands.

The Beach House

I arise early, drawn to bay window
Waves gently roll toward the shoreline that
we will later walk upon
when the sun rises;
as we follow whale spouts, not caring
how distant they are. We'll join
Curlews and Sanderlings, canines with their people in tow;
it'll be a merry celebration – a day at the beach.

But, for now, in the dawn light, I only know
the beauty of the crescent moon
paired closely with Venus
above the pier and it's lamps
reflecting onto incoming tide, and bending gracefully
past each column until
waves touch the shore.

Profile of eucalyptus frame northerly
view, while dragon-shaped hills
tumble down to the sea. The quiet of
this house is filled with slumbering
gems – my deeply loved friends.

I do not yet know that we will
see dolphins up close
as they feed near this pier,
gracing us with their presence
for long, lovely moments.

I do not yet know
how the joys, laughter and allure
of this weekend will buoy us always,
as constant as the early morning
tide.

Impressions

We sit on roofed front porch
with friends
relishing the first rain in
months

The smells, the sounds,
the atmosphere itself
hold us huddled and hypnotized
until the rain lightens

As the clouds part
a golden glow tops every tree
reflecting in the
dew drops and within
six sets of
enchanted eyes

Before the Rush

Early cool, early calm
Cat purring at my shoulder
Fridge humming

Sky starting to pink streak
Silhouette of ponderosas
Slender grace of cedars
Once again greet my gaze

The clock ticks toward
Time to get ready for work
But the cat has held me
Hostage

Climbing into my
Lap – her warmth, along with the
Wisps of steam rising from

My tea cup
Forcing me to
Cozy
Into the dawning
Of this day

Commuting at Dawn

In the moments before dawn
and after the rain,
the oak trees glowed

Though the air is not cold enough
for frost,
they look frosted

White, puffy, just short of
glittering ~
canopies shrouded in lifting fog

      all the recent gifts of moisture
      playing about
      bare, January branches

The light that proceeds
sunrise defines
the shapes

of my mystical
      morning
          commute

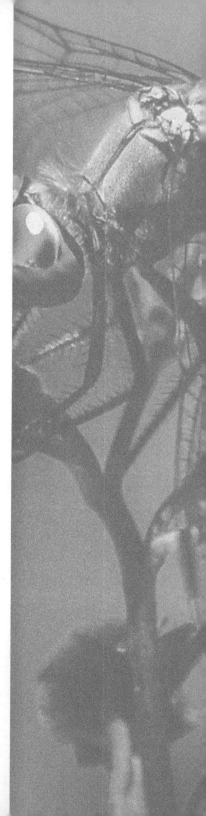

Sustenance

Lovely sunrise,
pink and purple lenticular clouds
gracing horizon
above Kirby ridge

Pines lining up like soldiers atop
cedar silhouettes fill in the
foreground
beyond our second story deck,
our treehouse
where we gaze at our
colorful world each day;
where we bask in sunbeams
in morning moments

Where we toast our neighbors
and their horses, goats and chickens
as we regroup in the evenings

Moments of peace and beauty
Sustain us

The clouds are hiding

the sun on this
early summer day, presenting
a calm to the end
of a rowdy school year.

Deep breath time.
Sit and relax body
and mind time.
Reflect; rejuvenate.

Thank you clouds for
slowing my pace.
You gently move
across the sky

Graceful, purposeful;
Free.

We met on the Mesa

　　　　many moons ago – so young
And high on life's beauty
And possibilities.

Our paths diverged and reconnected
Through the years; always picking
Up joyfully, sometimes tearfully,
Where we'd left off.

Hiking the canyon of our youth
Crossing the mesas and gullies
Of life's renderings
Always, always reconnecting
With some deep palpable glow.

My YaYa sister
My lovely friend

I hold you dearly
I hold you gently
In a magical space
Of time untouched
And love unlimited

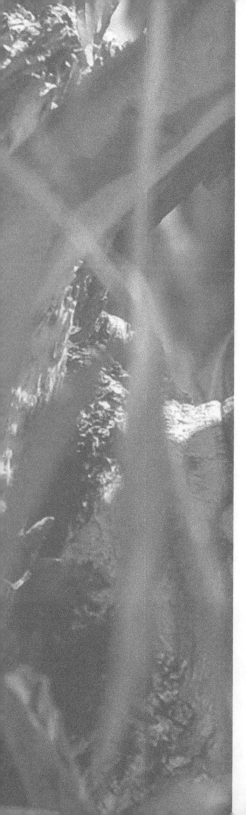

The thunder rolls...

      and love surrounds
everyone at the celebration of life
Ceremony

Scrub Jays fly over
as if wanting
to be a part of the remembrances
of an avid birder.
Someone who honored
and cherished them.
The humans tell
stories, read poems
Sing songs – sometimes with a
catch in their
voices.

Through laughter
and tears;
through music,
poetry and anecdotes;
we honor a life
well lived…
And the thunder rolls
And the light rain comes.
A hug from
Mother Nature

A whisper of loss –
yet love still here

What did I do to deserve

the Redbud's blush,
the plum trees concert
of bees on nascent blooms?

What did I do to deserve
the robins' melody as
the rising sun warms
my shoulder?

Of course, this is presuming
it's all for me!
This impossible beauty,
these brilliant systems
of growth and revolution

These cycles of life
all around me
and you
and us
What did we do to
deserve this?

Discerning

To know the color of redbud in spring,
to know the comfort of savory soup,
to feel the hug of a loving friend -
These are beyond seeing, beyond sight.

To know a child's unconditional love,
to know a teen's incomparable humor,
to comprehend an elder's wisdom -
These are beyond hearing, beyond sound.

A pair of geese lift off the pond,
a tree frog chortles to lure a mate,
Manzanita's bloom rose cups in season -
These things are certain; clear signs of promise.

To be conscious of beauty will lift our souls,
to be attentive to hearing beyond sound,
will uplift our communities -
To be mindful of others begins our response.

To the world that needs deliberate seeing
beyond sight; attentive hearing
beyond sound; and a knowing
beyond knowledge.

Up the Slough

After school, we went up the slough!
Kayaks swerving to and fro
from lack of practice
Seals shadowing from ocean launch,
playfully nose-bumping paddles
Herons and egrets noting our progress
a few lifting off with fanciful wingspans
Mallards and mergansers dabbling and diving
one edgy duck eye upon us

And, then, just around the bend, - the otters!
Babies on momma's
Some rolling friskily
Lounging and cuddling
We give them space
cameras clicking,
eyes adoring

So like us
in playfulness and parental love
endearing mammals of river
and sea

The wind chimes play

      a tune in D minor
while the Dogwood leaves
dance and sway

The wily blue sky holds
the winter-cold air,
but the sun is summer-warm
dazzling through my window

Sneaky how friends find out
minor key preference;
cunning how age brings
perception of simple things ~

the sun,
      the wind,
            the resonate
                    song
of caring comrades;
           life's notable nourishments

Sun-shower

A hard rain in the night
        was comforting in this dry land.
Daybreak brought cloud-play;
low stratus zooming southwest
while brushing yonder ridge;
higher cirro-cumulus leisurely heading
northeast, billowy edges, sunlit.

A mesmerizing morning
meditation folded into
a sun-shower!
Light steady rain as
Sun rays flourish.

The ridge disappears
behind descending fog
as the earth soaks in moisture,
we are quenched with beauty.

Who knew that
the day would begin
with such loveliness?
Take it with you, the breeze whispers;
allow it's nourishment,
feel it's enfoldment,
rest in nature's embrace
and carry on with
        contentment

Yosemite Sunset

Pale pink-orange mist floating
near sheer granite cliff face
in evening's fading light
Captivates

      until bright crescent moon
beckons across the valley
making itself known just above
Cathedral Spires

Such beauty, my heart cries,
such beauty!
Why are we so confused amid
such splendor?

Kindred Spirits

Moonlit nights and mountain tops,
serenely beautiful,
remind me
of you, my honored friends

Treks through alpine meadows
scrambling like goats
on scree
Berry-blue hands cupping
clear water from tarn

Peach melba sunsets
mingle with
stunning full-moon radiance

Marmot and ptarmigan chorus
as we perch on jagged peak
our senses utterly filled
with the splendor, the wonder
of our world

Moonlit nights and mountain tops,
serenely beautiful,
remind me
of you, my honored friends

Compare and Contrast

Costa Rican morning:
>   Tropical birdsong; exotic white throated magpie-jay
>   watching us watching him as waves gently
>   brush fine sand

Sierra foothill morning;
>   hazy from smoke; Robin sings "cheery-cheer-up" song,
>   neighbor hitting golf balls –
>   clic-bick

Costa Rican coffee- time:
>   howler monkey commotion, gecko landing on
>   a man's bald pate, iguana scurrying from pool to jungle,
>   ocean islands kissed with sunlight

Back in the mountains:
>   Tom turkeys parading through yard;
>   Finch nesting in gutter, pine needles sway
>   in gentle morning breeze

My mind drifts to Costa Rica where waves
>   crash onto the shore; where pelicans fly low on
>   their breakfast run and kisskadees
>   serenade the world

Woodpeckers on my house, pounding it home
>   that each place is unique;
>   each place fills me up

Cada lugar me llena de alegria.*

*Each place fills me with happiness

Shelter

Midnight rain comes
to the high country…
Gentle at first
then pounding into hail
with added light and sound show.

So much for sleep.

But I don't mind –
just smile and snuggle deeper
into my bag,
thankful for a good tent
and cozy sleeping pad.

For the dramatic storm
will bless this dry land
And, as it gentles once again,
will serenade me
back to slumber

LOVE GETS YOU THROUGH

everything,
doesn't it?
Through days, months
years…whatever it takes
Time, unimportant
insignificant, really
Love is there shaping
the psyche opening channels
for new awareness,
perception that's been lurking
just released
Like a little stick dam
Breaking with stream waters
Trickling over, through
cleansing, freeing
Elevating - opening
new possibilities for
further adventure
Downstream, upstream
Slipstream
Eddying then …SWOOsH!
On to new adventures in
Learning
Growth
Discernment
Possibilities
Probabilities
Twists and turns and oxbows and rapids and calm, gentle runs
into the big restful lake
which has it's own seasons

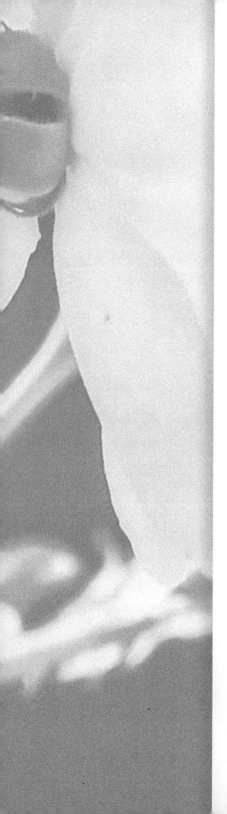

If a Rose can Blossom

> without much effort
> So can you; so can I

If a sunset can create
A daily masterpiece
> So can you; so can I

If watching a family of deer can
take away one's worries
> So it can for you; so it can for me

Glance at any part of nature's creations
Take in the beauty and structure,

Know you are part of the phenomenon
then, effortlessly ease into
> The you that you are
> The me that is me

Lakeside Observations

Osprey dips
And plucks a fish
From abundant waters

Above the shoreline
Bald eagle roams.
It's destination known
Only by one.
It's graceful flight
Admired by two.

Dusk deepens…

Loons call
In the night
Clear and mysterious
In the quiet glow
Of full moon's light.

A distant owl hoots as campfire embers
Slowly cool
Yet, we are warmed

By humble thoughts
Of our small part
In the consummate whole
Of an exquisite mystery.

A Mountain Blessing

Wishing you wildflower meadows,
big rocks to perch on,
Ravens to caw with,
Mountains to roam.

May you always have friends at the campfire;
Stories to warm,
plenty of black beans;
soft ground to lie upon.

May you have ears that will listen
to the mountain stream's song;
bidding you kindness,
refreshing your soul.

May you skip with the children,
feel the joy of their laughter;
open your eyes to the simple
stark beauty of stones.

May your heaven be here
in the wonders of now
and your joy be full
as the croaking toad.